Bound Together

Like the Grasses

Blessings, Deb Cooper

Happy reading,
Ann Niedringhaus

Bound Together

Like the Grasses

Poems by

Deborah Cooper
Candace Ginsberg
Ann Floreen Niedringhaus
Ellie Schoenfeld
Anne Simpson

Clover Valley Press, LLC
Duluth, Minnesota

Clover Valley Press, LLC
6286 Homestead Rd.
Duluth, MN 55804-9621
USA

Cover fine art print "Dune Grass" © 2013 by Joel Cooper
Cover design by Stacie Whaley, i.e. design

Printed in the United States of America on acid-free paper.

Library of Congress Control Number: 2013950499

ISBN: 978-0-9846570-7-0

ACKNOWLEDGMENTS

"A Stirring" ~ *Migrations*
"Some Day" ~ *Growing Down*
"Before" ~ *The Gods of Wild Things*
"Below," "Still," "We Could Be" ~ *Parallel to the Horizon*
"Daughters with Disabilities," "Lake Superior Fish" ~ *Life Suspended*
"Early Marriage: West Virginia" ~ *The Country Doctor Revisited*, earlier
    version in *North Coast Review* (Vol. 21, 2002)
"Swimming Lesson" ~ *The Comstock Review*
"Teenaged Girl" ~ *The Teacher's Voice*
"The Daughter" ~ *Kalliope*
"The Widow" ~ *Sidewalks*
"Vigils" ~ *Calyx*
"We All Wake to the Same Sun" ~ *Under the Bridges of America*

How We Wrote

Bound Together: Like the Grasses

For sixteen years, we have met monthly over dinner, sharing our lives, the mundane and the sacred, sharing our words. The evolution and bonding of a writing group remains a mystery. Ours grows out of an atmosphere of affirmation, raucous laughter, and gentle challenge.

Life stories, ordinary and profound experiences and insights, are shared. Distinct writing styles and philosophies express each individual's unique search for understanding, for a patch of ground to stand on in the wind.

Walking together through time and transitions, through the dark struggles, and the surprise of joy, has woven the scattered sands of our lives together, and given strength to each of our individual voices.

Deborah Cooper
Candace Ginsberg
Ann Floreen Niedringhaus
Ellie Schoenfeld
Anne Simpson

These things happen...
the soul's bliss
and suffering
are bound together
like the grasses.
— Jane Kenyon

CONTENTS

V.

VI.

VII.

VIII.

1.

I live my life in widening circles.

— Rainer Maria Rilke

THE HAWKS

The hawks let go with grace
full dips and swirls they ride
the current, the what is,
the now.
They ride it out.
They let go
of this place
this time.
A million golden leaves
wave them on,
sing them a traveling song.

— Ellie Schoenfeld

EVERY TURNING OF THE WORLD

The seasons turning
and the hours,
the hands of the clock,
the pages of the calendar.

The earth turns
and the tides;
the water tumbling
in the creek,
turning the rocks
to perfect orbs,
to eggs.

The seeds in your hands
become the garden,
become the harvest,
become the soup
in the bowl in your hands.

The leaves turn
and the geese, crossing the sky.
We turn as one in sleep.

Rain turns to snow
turning the fields to light;
the rush of the creek
to a hush,
the hush to silence.

My brother turns to mist.
My brother's body turns
to stone, to ash.
I turn to face the darkness.
You turn me back again.

Nana's wedding dress
has turned to tatters.
Granddad's flannel shirts
have turned to scraps.
My hands can turn these remnants
to a quilt

to wrap the baby,
turning in the womb
of the daughter,
who is turning into a mother.

The dusk turns into night,
the night to morning.
The wind turns into song,
the bells, to birds.
The flowers turn their faces
to the sun.
I turn my face to you.

— Deborah Cooper

TEENAGED GIRL

You are a window leaning up against a tree,
a door lying at the bottom of a ravine.
You are somewhere between liquid and solid –
slowly slipping from my grasp.

You are buffed, tweezed, shaved, powdered,
penciled-in and tinted. You paint yourself
into a corner, and even when the paint is dry,
refuse to walk out.

You seek out high places unprotected
while I stand below, barely able to watch.
I strain to read the direction signs you follow,
but they are in a language I no longer know.

— Ann Floreen Niedringhaus

AN UNREFINED NORTHERN POEM

There is nothing refined
about the way the water
meets the shore —
all that pounding and lapping
and the leaving of broken glass,
driftwood, a rusty can.
No pearls here, no shells to hold
to your ear to hear secrets.
If you are holding bread
to cast onto the waters
the seagulls will swoop in
to divert that good intention
to a more primal impulse,
a primal hunger.
Everything here is hungry.
This is not an
elegant well-behaved place.
This water will break
your boat in two,
will suck the living warmth
out of your body in minutes
and throw your broken bones
back to the shore
where a vulture,
who has never learned table manners,
is waiting to eat.

— Ellie Schoenfeld

BAY

We plod with Wellies
across the sandy muck
of a mud flat
unexpectedly revealed
by the drought of spring.

The pages of history
spread beneath our feet.

A whale oil lamp – lost
overboard in a nor'easter.
A Buster Brown shoe – kicked off
in hopes of shiny patent leather.
Rusted bed springs – worn out
from rowboat passion.
A pistol – tossed with empty magazine
after he was discovered.

— Candace Ginsberg

IMAGINE

I am standing at the sink scrubbing dishes,
when she walks by on the sidewalk below –
the little woman, hugging her big black plastic bag.
She looks up at my window
longing for a lighted room and a warm meal.

In a kitchen that could feed multitudes, I cook
my solitary supper while she
walks to the crowded shelter down the hill
where she will stand in line for hours
to get a bowl of soup and a cot.

How could she and I ever understand each other?
How does the lion lie down with the lamb,
Republican compromise with Democrat,
how do the Arab and the Christian and the Jew
stand together on God's holy mountain?

She may be diminished by hopes too small
and I hobbled by dreams too big,
but I bow my head over the kitchen sink
and try to imagine peace in all the earth,
with room for her at the inn.

— Anne Simpson

A FRIEND TELLS ME THAT EVERY SOUL HAS TO INVENT THEIR OWN VERSION OF THE WHEEL

For the longest time
I favored a triangle.
I liked thinking about pyramids
and how they are purported to contain
paranormal powers.
It made me feel
foreign and exotic
as though I were filled
with golden treasures,
hidden mysteries.
But every time I climbed
up to the apex
I fell down
and, frankly, it hurt.
I started thinking about how I was
no spring chicken, started worrying
about breaking a hip.
I moved on

to a square.
Something so tidy and organized
about a square, it appealed
to my Germanic background.
And at first it was good
but then, as with all things
tidy and organized,
I couldn't sustain it.
I kept finding myself

feeling trapped, sitting in a corner
thinking about what I had done.
No one had to tell me
that everything I had done
was wrong.
Next

I turned to the spiral,
the spinning Sufi dancer,
the new green fern unfurling,
the swirling of stories
ever outward.
But the spinning got out of control.
The constant movement
made me dizzy, the vortex
kept stirring up
one difficult thing after another
until I was in danger of being
completely consumed in the chaos.
I started to lose track
of the original point,
could never
get back to the beginning
of anything.
Then finally, after an absurdly long time,
I spotted

the circle.

The circle
with its smooth edges
and its sense
of being full and complete.
I liked the way I could keep
going back over
the same territory,
the way I could see
how the trees I'd planted
earlier in the desolate valleys
grew bigger and changed
everything around them,
nourished things
I still don't know the names of.
The understory is alive
and always rustling.
I am never sure
what will suddenly rise up
and try to kill me
or try to help me.
Everything there is
is in a circle
and everything there is
is what the soul needs to keep
rolling along on its road.
So I'm going to stay

with the idea of the wheel as circle.

I'm going
to roll around
as though I am a marble
in a game where I don't know
the rules,
a planet
in an undiscovered solar system,
or a single shiny sequin,
just one small piece
of an enormous undulating mosaic
of lights.
I'm going
to keep moving
like a round unloosed bumper car
and see what happens
when I bump into you.

— Ellie Schoenfeld

II.

Things happen anyway, whether we are aware or not.

— Denise Levertov

THROUGH THE NIGHT

The orange cat dreams
of the damaged bird

the damaged bird,
of flight.

The baby's whimpering
wakes no one

but enters the dream
of the nun
in the narrow room
on the other side of town.

A woman turns her back
to the man who breathes beside her,
miles away.

A girl and a boy meet
at the edge of the woods,
embrace.

The bear sleeps dreamlessly.
An owl rises from a white pine.

A man lies down
on his wife's vacant side
of the bed,

last trace of perfume
on the pillow.

A woman
in a nursing home
clutches a rosary.

Her grandson
in Afghanistan
clutches a gun.

A prisoner dreams
of home.
A young girl dreams
of running.

A mother cries out
in her sleep;
her husband,
without waking,
takes her hand.

A woman
with a mass of auburn curls
makes tea,
and prays for daybreak.

A soldier dreams
of loosening
a woman's hair.

An old man
in a coma
drifts away,
slips into the dreams
of the daughter
he's not spoken to in years.

Something is mended
as she sleeps.

A man in a cell
dreams of flight,
like the damaged bird.

The orange cat stretches
in the day's first light.

The sun grazes the horizon.

— Deborah Cooper

MILKY WAY

Small hands laid the wounded dog
upon a nest of old blankets
hidden high in the sandy dune grasses.
There, four children kept watch –

Thick carnelian blood oozed from the dog's snout –
her ribs moved with her rapid breaths
her eyes glazed and un-seeing.

Above, the cold obsidian night sky was painted
with a dense swathe of brilliant jewels –
a broad brush stroke never noticed before.

The dog's and the children's breath could be seen
in the crisp air – little puffs of white mist.
But her breaths grew slower, and,
finally – still.

They hovered, uncertain, at this
their first death watch,
taking in the Milky Way –
the spaciousness of the universe
the quietude of death.

      — Candace Ginsberg

CIRCLE OF STARS

Far from the city,
the little ones settled at last,
we step into the night

try to trace the patterns
in the sky's elaborate
needlepoint of stars.

Here, then there,
one slips across
the glittered dome,
making music of the silence.

I claim a constellation,
whisper a prayer
made of the names
of the dead

made more of praise
than sorrow.

You wake the children,
carry them outside,
starlight reflected
in their faces.

           — Deborah Cooper

PERCHANCE WE DREAM

Sometimes sleep sneaks up and clubs you over the head...
after dinner, for instance, when you are sitting in your favorite chair
with a good novel in your hands
and just this one night to finish it
before your book club meets tomorrow.

Other times, the touch is so gentle that your eyelids barely close
and all night you watch the numbers drift
across the face of your clock
as the wrongs you've done or had done unto you
march across your mind

or you worry about the dear children
you have damaged for life by negligent parenting
or a project you are working on
which you will never finish
given all the duly noted failures of your past.

You soak in lemon baths,
drink warm milk with honey,
inhale lavender
and wonder when it is too late to take a pill
or too early to get up.

Maybe the moon conspires against you.
Maybe she is in secret negotiations with pharmaceuticals
or the cosmetic industry
and that is why the hairs of your head, so carefully numbered,
turn grey after midnight

and why it is only on the days you want to look your best
that you awake with black circles under puffy eyes
and why, on one wonderful night,
when your sleep is blissfully sound
the moon has the decency to hide her head.

— Anne Simpson

WHO SAID

1.

Bill Holm said
"You cannot blaspheme water."

But you can build mines
and fill them with copper sulfides
and poison everyone
who needs a drink.
You can trade in thousands of years
of clean water for thirty pieces
of silver, for a few years of "good jobs."

You can
but you don't have to.

2.

The Mad Hatter
had a pretty good job
so he didn't ask pesky questions
about health and safety,
he trusted that the industry
had taken the necessary steps
regarding the mercury.
Now he fills his days crazy
boiling poisoned water
for the tea party.

— Ellie Schoenfeld

LAKE SUPERIOR FISH

Only the hardiest remain
        growing slow
plain   gray   still

They concentrate toxin
        in the fat
they collect for warmth
against the constant cold

They learn to follow
        warm muddy effluents
flowing in from streams

They cross vast open spaces
        to seek narrow bands
of vegetation near islands
where for a while they
        feast and revel
in ease of plenty

But winter eventually comes
        and when it does
they hang like stones suspended
        and triumph
by merely surviving

— Ann Floreen Niedringhaus

WE HAVE NO IDEA

We wander in the Spring
through the uncountable shades of green,
slightly lost.
We open our mouths
and turtles leap
into the watery ditches.

We try to sing
but all our mouths want
to do is kiss.

We have no idea
what the sun will
call back to life,
his warm fingers digging deep
into the winter
which is melting away
inside of us.
Elemental songs reach
the sleeping bear
who is dreaming about a time
filled with every kind
of fruit and berry,
delicious and dripping,
the scent sliding sweet
under the nostrils,
across the soul.

What has been asleep
is waking up.

Bird songs waft
between our blood cells.
Somewhere a nest
is holding something
about to hatch.

We open our mouths to see
what will happen next.
We move
from one kind of green
to another
just wanting
to taste everything.

— Ellie Schoenfeld

III.

So much that can neither be written nor kept inside.

— Tomas Tranströmer

THE SHAPE OF SILENCE

*"The absence of something has a shape
that can be recognized."*
— Jane Miller

For months,
the piano waits.
He is too ill to play

and then, one day
he can again

for twenty minutes,
then an hour,
some days, two.

The music he's creating
he entitles 'Wreck'

the final, haunting
half-a-piece
he'll leave us...

and he leaves us.

His absence takes the shape
and weight of silence,
of the musical notation: 'Rest'

a silence that is meant to be
a pause,
before the melody resumes...

but it does not.

— Deborah Cooper

DAUGHTERS WITH DISABILITIES

I can't write about
    your lurching gait, awkward, unbalanced;
    the miracle: you rarely fall;
    the work it takes for you to talk, processing
    what to say and how to form it.

I can't write about
    how I used to watch other families
    wondering if life was
    as easy for them as it appeared.

I can't write about
    the way I become invisible when I am with you
    as strangers avert their eyes or stare
    unblinking, as if we can't see them gawk.

I can't write about
    how unexpected pain returns when friends
    tell of children's weddings, achievements,
    of grandchildren – pain as raw and briny
    as at diagnosis, but momentary.

I can't write about
    my disappointment in others
    and myself
    when we presume we know
    what you can and cannot do.

I can't write about
  your vulnerable walking in the world
  unique
  oblivious to my fears for you.

— Ann Floreen Niedringhaus

CHEMO SIDE EFFECTS

Your mouth tastes like metal,
your bottom lip is erupting in sores,
you nibble on soda crackers to settle your queasy stomach.
Your hands are numb
your hair thin and straight, you need a bath...
when one of the people you love most in the world
calls to ask if you'd like company.

Do you express delight and gratitude?
Do you scoop up newspapers lying about the living room,
jump into the shower,
chill wine or start the coffee?

You do not.

You mumble an excuse,
wipe your eyes with the palm of your hand
and go back to your book.
Unable to concentrate,
feeling more lonely than you did before,
you are pinned to that over-stuffed chair
by the very pride that may help you to heal.

— Anne Simpson

BELOW

May it float underwater,
    may it stay
    submerged –
this news, this loss.

Then maybe
    I can immerse myself
    in my hopes,
never need to emerge.

Below
    edges are softened
    outlines unclear.
In dappled shade
    there is even
    a chance
it has not
    happened at all.

           — Ann Floreen Niedringhaus

THIS TWILIGHT

As a boy
the quiet man
with silver hair

had loved the mystery
of the Mass

the songs and stories
of his Sunday morning classes.

He'd sung "this little light of mine"
in his clear, true voice...

before he'd reached the age
of un-belonging.

After that, he'd lived
a hidden life

showing the world
only a practiced portion.

How is it then
this quiet man

upon the bench
along the peopled path

in this aching-blue of twilight

takes the hand
of the man
who sits beside him

by his side in sickness
and in health

in times of burden
and of bounty

the man who
in this moment
does not turn or speak

but simply lays his head
upon the shoulder

of the one he's loved
for over forty years.

A light shines in them
and around them

and it is good.

— Deborah Cooper

IV.

It has become too dangerous to continue as we have.

— Louis Jenkins

THE VERY BAD IDEA

It was a very bad idea.

A herd of elephants
trampled it,
a kindle of kittens
set it on fire,
a band of gorillas
played protest music,
a mischief of mice
made trouble for it,
an implausibility of gnus
couldn't believe it,
a tower of giraffes
looked down on it,
a litter of pigs
threw it out the window
of a moving car,
a sleuth of bears
uncovered its secrets,
a string of ponies
ran it up the flagpole
and pointed out
that no one saluted
the very bad idea.

It was a very bad idea.

A troubling of goldfish
worried themselves sick about it,

a bed of clams
slept on it,
a smack of jellyfish
whacked it around,
a riddle of eels
asked a lot of questions about it,
a bed of oysters
joined the bed of clams
and made strange bedfellows
in the fight against
the very bad idea.

It was a very bad idea.

A skein of geese
unraveled it,
a charm of finches
tried to make it disappear,
a murmuration of starlings
muttered to anyone who would listen,
a mob of emus
got out of control about it,
a murder of crows
tried to kill it,
an ostentation of peacocks
turned up their beaks at it,
a watch of nightingales
kept their eyes on it,

a congregation of birds
prayed for it to be gone,

It was a very bad idea.

A cloud of gnats
rained on it,
a rumba of rattlesnakes
danced it out of town,
a colony of ants
colonized it to death,
a culture of bacteria
made it taboo,
a parliament of owls
ruled against it
and the very bad idea
was executed immediately.

— Ellie Schoenfeld

GUILTY CONSCIENCE

He stands at the intersection of here and anywhere,
these sultry summer days –
weak, damp, downcast –
but always with the strength to raise his eyes
and look right into mine
when I am forced to stop,
as if he dares me to proceed when the light turns green
without noticing him.

I look away.
I curse the light for being slow to change,
I curse him for making me uncomfortable,
I curse myself for thinking
There but for the grace of God...

There is nothing graceful about this situation,
and I don't know where to find God in it.

Renounce all you have, says Jesus,
Go, sell what you own and give the money to the poor.
But then I become the same burden on society as this stranger.
Give a cup of water, visit prison, clothe and feed...
But I am one and they are legion.

Donate to homeless shelters,
serve at the soup kitchen,
stock food shelves...
Yes, Lord, I can do that!

But, meanwhile, here You are
standing right in front of me
holding up a floppy cardboard sign
OUT OF WORK
LOST MY HOME
and I am idling in air-conditioned comfort,
windows rolled up,
foot resting on the gas pedal,
ready to pull away as soon as the light changes.

— Anne Simpson

THEY ARE TIRED OF THE POOR

They are tired of the poor
and of how they stay
poor, get poorer.
They are tired of the sick
and of how they keep
getting sick.
They are tired
of people who need help.
They are tired of it.
They are tired of problems
which are not fixed
in the time span
of a made-for-TV movie.
They miss John Wayne.
Some of them buy guns
and imagine
they are John Wayne.
They do not miss
John Lennon.

— Ellie Schoenfeld

THE WATCH

T'ick t'ick t'ick
the watch, like a pulse,
keeps track of the beat

the beat of the drum
announcing the passage
of yet another
soldier to the grave

the grave with the white cross
like all the others
in line after line
row upon row
        stretching to the horizon

a horizon that just days ago
lit up in a glorious sunrise
upon a land torn by war
and divided by hate

a hate so strong
that bodies are splattered –
shrapnel splots on walls and posts
        on cars and faces

the faces of children, soldiers and civilians
        their eyes widened with shock
as the energy strikes them, too
        sucks the life force from within

and leaves behind the
t'ick t'ick t'ick
of another bomb
tied to another watch
strapped to another pulse

— Candace Ginsberg

HORRENDOUS CERTAINTY

Title phrase from Michael Dennis Browne

Whatever the opinion,
whether I agree or not,
when I sense within another's words,
or my own,
absolute surety

a part of me freezes
starting deep,
and the chill spreads
to my furthest extremities.

There it is:
that horrendous certainty.
    A door closes.
    A back is turned.
    A word of betrayal is spoken.

It's so comfortable
being right. Then
I can take the next steps:
    Stop listening.
    Buttress arguments on my side.
    Find fellow believers.
    Dismiss any merit
        in alternative points of view.
Now I can do anything.

       — Ann Floreen Niedringhaus

THERE IS NOTHING WE WILL NOT LET THE BOMBS DO

That night the bombs
did not burst in air.
They burst
in the house. In the house
with the sleeping children.

Bombs are like that.
They fail
to distinguish between thin air
and thin flesh,
can't tell the difference
between someone who is trying
to kill them
and a mother
nursing her child.
That night the bombs

did not burst in air.
That night the bombs
burst in the house.
The bombs burst
in the house full
of children
who were sleeping.
Of children who were sleeping.
Sleeping.
Children.
Bursting.

— Ellie Schoenfeld

WE ALL WAKE TO THE SAME SUN

the woman in the brownstone;
the man in the trailer
at the end of a dirt road;
the boy sleeping in the dumpster,
seeking refuge from the cold.

We live and move in this same
circle of light,
crossing the sky and sea,
the walls and barricades
and borders.

We whisper the same prayers
in a thousand tongues...
Peace.
The safety of our loved ones.
Peace.

We all shelter the same
small flame of hope.
We all come to know
the weight of grief.
We hold our children close.
We hold the old ones.

We see beauty
in a single yellow flower...
in a field or in a child's hand;
through the barred window

of a cell.

We hear beauty
in the music of a nightingale,
a lark.

All over the world
we join our voices,
singing the way open
in every language,
singing the shackles free.

In different countries,
bells or drums
call us to prayer.
We bow.
We kneel.
We face the four directions…

the same praise in our mouths;
the same needs in our hearts.

Night falls the same way everywhere,
the deepening blue,
the dusk,
the dark…
upon the hungry and the fed,
the loved,
the lonely.

We dream the same dreams everywhere,
inside a tent,
a penthouse
or a high-rise.

Sleep beneath the same soft moon,
the same tossed scattering of stars.

We all wake to the same sun.

— Deborah Cooper

V.

We are made to persist. That's how we find out who we are.

— Tobias Wolff

VIGILS

The second robin stands on the driveway
as I open the automatic garage door.
I raise a curtain on her vigil. I failed
to figure out how the first robin died yesterday
in my garage. I simply found him there
and dumped him unceremoniously
into the gray plastic trash can by the door.

Now the second robin – unmoving, unstartled –
stands guard. She has fixed her gaze
on the inside of the garage. She looks
through me to the place where she
must have last seen her mate. And I wait,
unable to drive away, forced to watch her
and think my troubled, admiring thoughts.

— Ann Floreen Niedringhaus

SHE LOOKS FOR HIM

She looks for him
in the home they never shared
forgetting, every time she opens the front door,
that he will not be there to welcome her.

Separate quarters.
Independent living.
He in a nursing home, she in a modern condo,
far from the community that has nourished them.

There is no sound except the key turning in the lock,
not even a tap... tap of the dog's nails on the hardwood floor.
Their old companion is gone –
no wiggling, wagging tail,
no one to talk to, no warm body to touch.

She turns on the classical music station,
opens the window to late summer breeze.
She will close it soon
against the rush hour traffic,
her silence gone outside in.

She remembers the country,
leaves just turning,
walks in the woods,
long quiet sits by the Lake.

Visiting him today,
she sat and held his hand

as the quiet seeped into his mind, his limbs.
She wonders if he knew that she was there,
if his soul remembers…

She feeds him, strokes and comforts
as she tries to find him in a smile,
a faded photograph,
a shaft of light through the opening door.

— Anne Simpson

THE DAUGHTER

Now that he is dwindling,
going down
for the third time,
thrashing
in the tangle of the sheets,
she comes from far away
to care for him.

She wipes his face,
tips tiny sips of water
in the sunken cave of the mouth
that spit the battering words at her;
washes the hands
that sent her running
for the woods.

Once, she lay
beneath the maple tree
all night,
prayed for a fire
to come and take him.

Today, she rubs his feet
and scrubs the kitchen
of the trailer
where he's lived for years
alone,
at the dead end
of a dirt road;

hauls in the wood
that keeps him warm.
She is making things right,

repairing,
in the only way she knows,
the holes
he's left inside her.

— Deborah Cooper

THE WIDOW

She opens and closes her lips slowly
    like a tropical fish
flutters her tissue like a chiffon fin.

With a sideways nod of her head
    and a swallow
she raises her eyes reluctantly to the pulpit.

Muffled words float around her.

beloved husband

                death

    darkness

never failing love

          child of God

   loss

       consolation

           separation

When the murmur stops, she rises,
    wobbling, and begins
her swim against the weight of water.

             — Ann Floreen Niedringhaus

IN POETRY CLASS AT THE JAIL
DEREK TALKS ABOUT THE MOON

The moon he can see
through the window of his cell

for seven lucky minutes
every night it's clear.

Then Justin talks about the moon
that rose above the barn

on the farm of his seventh
foster family

the way it soothed
his loneliness.

Bart writes a poem about the memory
of moonlight upon snow

when he was only nine,
first time he ran away.

Josh recalls a winter
on the streets, fifteen…

the coldest nights, spent
huddled in a dumpster.

We write in silence then.

When they're led back to their blocks
for lockdown, I head home.

A pale moon sails
the darkening canopy of sky

from wide horizon
to horizon.

— Deborah Cooper

NOVEMBER

November, this bleak emptiness

then suddenly I see

the trees, transformed
to windows.

Through the stark bare limbs,
once thick with green,
I see the rolling blue of water.

Wild geese, crossing the sky,
weave through the branches.

And in the night,
where once was darkness,
a kaleidoscope of stars.

A veiled moon rises.

— Deborah Cooper

VI.

... and the world constantly pitches its tent anew.

— Tomas Tranströmer

BEGIN

The first breath
and each successive one,
awakenings

twenty-thousand risings
of the sun

each subtle shift,
each incremental turning

the swift descent...

the slightest lifting
of the dark.

The bend in the road,
the key in the lock,
or the door closing.

Each accommodation
of the heart.

The first words
on the page

on the first day
of a new year

or any other day.

— Deborah Cooper

OUR BIRTHDAYS CAME

Our birthdays came –
but you did not.
Each year
with the faithfulness of seasons
you returned to share yourself with me.
But now, this year,
that sharing is done.

Sometime in May
you looked ahead and said,
"I must spread my wealth in new ways."
Perhaps still with old friends and loves
but on an unfamiliar path.

"I am ready," you declared.
Keep your needles, your bags of blood,
and let me run unfettered
to that new country
where breath will be restored,
acquaintances renewed
and a warm welcome prepared
for those next in line.

— Candace Ginsberg

ON THE LAKEWALK

They are sitting on our bench –
the one on the deck that juts out over the lake –
the small white-haired woman and the old man
bending his good ear toward her,
his arm around her shoulder.

Maybe they are remembering days like this,
the lake smooth as glass,
or maybe they recall storms with waves threatening
and high enough to engulf their perch.

Our ghosts sit in their laps
as generations past fold into ours
all wrapped in light fog
words floating lightly over the waters,
mist at the horizon.

— Anne Simpson

A STIRRING

The house you live in
is the house at the edge
of the woods.

You are forever looking out.

The woods are made of light
and shadow

the trees
toss the breeze
to one another

toss the birds
into the sky

always, a stirring
in the underbrush.

In the night
the trees are hung with stars

and you can hear the owl
wonder

as you wonder

some nights,
the keening of the wolves...

you understand this too.

Mornings,
tea warming your hands,
you stand at the window

and watch the day begin

and every morning
there is something new.

You will not turn away
until you've found it

or until it has found you.

All night, you dream
you move into the woods,
taking only what you'll need

a sack of apples
and a candle
and a quilt

a pen,
a book of empty pages.

— Deborah Cooper

AFTER LABOR DAY

There is a new feel to the air, a new slant of light,
an energy tinged with sadness
as trees will be tinged red and yellow
before they catch fire
and leave us with ash-grey November.

In this short burst of time
I feel an urgency to make my whole life worthwhile,
not to wither and turn brown and fall unnoticed
but to blaze with glory –
to be reckless, remarkable, magnificent.

So far, my most heroic deed has been to sort the closet.

I pack away sandals, get out the sensible shoes
and exchange cotton for wool.
With this new currency I want to buy time
as if I could keep the cold away
by being prepared for it.

As if, by knowing I will die,
I could be as beautiful as the innocent trees.

— Anne Simpson

HOPE MOVES UPON THE WATERS

It might be terror
that propels us.
It might be hunger
or despair.

But it is hope
that bears us.

Hope moves upon the waters.

And, though the threads unfurl
across the distances,
they do not break

the threads that bind us...
to our landscape,
to our language,
to a loved one's face.

Hope moves upon the waters

in the shape of a ship,
in the shape
of a desperate raft...

a lone figure in a river
on a moonless night.

Hope moves upon the waters.

— Deborah Cooper

UNLEASHED

Unleashed
the jib whips across the bow
and snaps
into place on the leeward side

the coaming
tilts hard down
barely blocking
the white foamed seas
from the cockpit and crew

high above
the mainsail bows the mast
as lines creak, shrouds groan,
and the tiller
quivers in response

A fiercely hot summer gale
streaks across the icy waters
creating its own Hi's and Lo's

The sailors are but leaves
tossed about
within this whirling dervish
on a planet
spinning with delight.

— Candace Ginsberg

VII.

... each day a treasured unimportance.

— William Stafford

CHICKEN FARMER BARBIE

You won't find
Chicken Farmer Barbie
at K-Marts or at the Malls.
This Barbie is only available
through your local CSA
or Whole Foods Co-op.
She has a pink pitchfork
and is wearing an outfit
woven of organically grown flax.
The seeds of that plant
are included for you to sprinkle
on your morning granola,
which is also included
if you buy batteries.
She carries a basket of grit
which she strews for the chickens
who are free-range, of course.
When the grit is gone
she fills the basket
with an assortment
of pastel-colored eggs,
variously sized.
She likes to spend the winter
thumbing through the chicken catalog
but she always winds up ordering
the same thing – the variety pack
plus a few extra of the Polish.
She loves the Polish because they look
like they are wearing

elaborate feather hats
and they sashay
like movie stars from the 1930s
missing only a marabou-edged dressing gown
and a long elegant cigarette holder
to complete the image
though this Barbie would certainly never
let any of her chickens
smoke.

— Ellie Schoenfeld

PICNIC

In a far corner of the park two brothers,
their shirts off, bodies glistening,
kick a sullen soccer ball
while their family
nestles under a tree to grill supper.

Their voices are choked by heat,
the air shimmers around them. Below us
the sluggish river is tucked under a blanket of fog.
Gratefully, we find a patch of shade,
a table with benches and a hilltop breeze.

We nibble fruit and cold chicken,
drink glass after glass of iced tea.
Our talk is lazy... musing about life,
memories, the state of the world...
We won't solve anything today.

As dark comes on, we pack our basket,
leaving scraps of conversation on the table.
I sweep them into my pocket to assemble later,
on a clear fall day,
into something I'll wish we had said.

— Anne Simpson

THANK YOU POEM

Thank you
for the red sequin
that you found
on the floor
in one of the places
you played
when you played
Vegas.
The red sequin
that you put
in your wallet
to bring to me
for a present
but that vanished
like a magic act into thin air
between there and here.
I like to think of it
rolling around in the world,
having adventures,
rising up like a sunrise
in someone's field of vision,
occasionally getting picked up
and held onto for a little while.
I like to think of it
slipping away again and again
in a Liberace-esque fairy tale
lighting the way back
to a sparkly future.
I like to think of it

during a dull meeting
or when someone is trying
to sell me something,
sort of like they tell dancers
to let their eyes
keep coming back
to one spot while spinning
to avoid getting dizzy.
I like to come back to
that bright spot,
the esteemed gift
of an unlikely red sequin
on the floor
that found you
in one of the places you played
so that you could
bring the idea of it
back to me.

          — Ellie Schoenfeld

THE BUDDHA LEANS BACK

The Buddha leans back
and contemplates the dawn,
the way the streaks of pink
remind him of stalks of rhubarb
merging with a strawberry sun
to set the daily fire.

The Buddha leans back
and contemplates rhubarb,
the pink stalks like long fingers
longing for the sweetness
of somebody's mouth.

The Buddha leans back
and contemplates the wind
as it rustles through
the rhubarb leaves
and makes them wave
like fan dancers,
like prayer flags.

The Buddha leans forward
and begins the ceremony
of lowering the fork to the pie.
He contemplates the colors
which reprise the sunrise.

He raises the fork to his mouth
and wishes all beings could be
so lucky. He savors
the auspicious sweet.

— Ellie Schoenfeld

A LITTLE ROOM
After 'Daystar' by Rita Dove

She wanted a little room for thinking.
Or better yet, a little room
for daydreaming,
seamlessly and undisrupted.
Perhaps a piano too.
She loved the quiet movements best,
'pianissimo.'

The wish came to her
while she was ironing her husband's shirts,
one for each day of the week.
Potatoes boiling over on the stove.
The children's fighting waking up
the baby from his nap.

She wanted a little room
for dreaming.
And a little time,
a pocket here, a snippet there.
Maybe, occasionally,
a whole entire morning
or an afternoon.

She wanted a little room of her own
for daydreaming.
Perhaps a single window
on one wall.
Perhaps a single tree
outside the window.

Every now and then, a bird…
the only company she'd need.

She wanted a little room of her own
for music and for dreaming,
a room with a hidden door
that no one else
would ever find.

— Deborah Cooper

AFTER THE POETRY WORKSHOP

My suitcase stands empty in the guest room,
jeans and T-shirts whirl in the washer,
fresh strawberries, milk, lettuce, and roasted chicken
stock the refrigerator; I picked them up on my way home.

I am settling in —
dusting, watering the plants,
reeling my mind back to the city,
landing it near my body.

But the country lingers in the smell of campfire,
in pine cones and the grandfather rock
I place on the mantle,
in scraps of paper — confetti on my desk —

in my resolution to write and read
every day
from now on
forever and ever...

as soon as I sort through the pile on the kitchen counter:
bills and letters, newspapers, catalogs,
and the voice messages
and the email —

a tsunami that threatens to shrink
my king-sized determinations to grocery and "to do" lists,
as if poems were handkerchiefs
to be ironed flat and neatly folded away.

— Anne Simpson

THIS POEM

This poem
is a little paper boat
floating in a river full
of moonlight and undulating fish,
slowly making its way
to you.
This poem
is the breath held
in a room lit only
by cakelight,
in those moments
before the wish is made,
before the candles go dark.
This poem
is your fondest wish
coming true.

This poem
dances through the ethers
in three-quarter time
to waltz with you
on a rainy night.
This poem
is a blanket
that covers you.
This poem
is an origami bird
carefully folded and gliding
into your sleep

where you are having
a sweet dream
about floating
in a little paper boat
while under the water
iridescent fish
tremble in the moonlight.

— Ellie Schoenfeld

VIII.

We live forward and understand backward.

— Soren Kierkegaard

IT MIGHT BEGIN

It might begin

>　with the rumble of a foghorn
>　or the calling of a loon,
>　the distant whistle of a train.

It might begin

>　with the scent of burning leaves,
>　the unleashed perfume
>　of the lilacs.

Today, it is the way
the empty swing
sways in the breeze.

>　　— Deborah Cooper

HINDSIGHT

Looking back, you understand
he wasn't trying to ignore you or annoy,
he wanted to remember your answer
to the question he asked over and over again...

Looking back, you understand
the brawny fear he wrestled but couldn't name,
limping and alone in the dark,
and you are awed by the courage it took
to grab on to life as it slipped through his fingers.

You understand that friends and family pulled away
because they didn't know
what to do, what to say,
didn't want to see what dementia looked like –
as if it were contagious.

What you can't understand, looking back,
is how his mind learned to accept its degradation
and his spirit, to the very end,
could radiate with love.

— Anne Simpson

OBJECTS IN MIRROR ARE CLOSER THAN THEY APPEAR...

For what we've loved
and left behind

or lost,
resides in us.

The swell of the sea
lives in the deep breath

the mountains,
in the mind's eye

a mother's hand,
in the soft palm of our own

a father's voice,
in the hollow of the ear

a missed child,
in the cradle of the chest.

All that we've loved
and left behind

or lost,
resides in us.

— Deborah Cooper

FRIENDSHIP

Each South Dakota summer in the upstairs
boys' bedroom, the Fourth of July rodeo
would come to him through open, screened window.
Waves of words, backstopped by broader roar
of crowd response, lit in his brain flashes
of the hump-backed Brahma bull charging
a prancing clown, a wiry cowboy perched on
the hoof-launched bronco.
                              So when he heard
his friend describe a Brooklyn balcony
off Bedford Avenue near Ebbets Field, where cheers
for the Dodgers rose and fell, where random words pierced
distant din giving clues to how the day
would end, the South Dakotan recognized
the sense of boyhood and of longing that they shared.

                        — Ann Floreen Niedringhaus

SENIOR MOMENTS

Like clouds snagged in bare branches,
words pause, then drift away,
dislodged by the slightest breeze

and I search the open sky
for those wisps of wisdom
that were tipping my tongue just moments ago,

but they have evaporated into the atmosphere
only to return
in a sudden shower

watering my parched brain
sometime
when I least expect them.

— Anne Simpson

CHRISTMAS BLIZZARD

Morning coffee by candlelight
by tree light
by the wild symphony
of wind and snow swirling and pelting –
everything wrapped and rapt
in that suite.
Icy crystals strewn
like broken ornaments,
a chandelier of stars
fallen from the heavens,
light laid down and out
at the feet of everything.

I contemplate the unnamable mysteries,
the things I hold dear
here in the mostly dark.
They flicker in

and out

like shooting stars,
the refrains and echoes
of ancient songs
they illuminate
temporary paths
through the storming dark.

The rising sun
unties its red ribbons

slowly.

It unveils
an invitation to unwrap
to open to the gift
of everything which is
at all times
being
given.

— Ellie Schoenfeld

IX.

Time flows through us like water.
The past and the dead speak through us.

— Marge Piercy

SANCTUARY

Close the door softly.
Let pictures hang straight on the walls,
let gentle dust preserve the piles on his desk.
You will visit this room again.

You will enter quietly,
open the shades,
sink deep into his worn leather chair.
Rest your head

and let the tears come.
You will not be afraid or angry here.
You will feel his hand resting in yours,
you will smell his pipe.

— Anne Simpson

RELIQUARY

In the woods,
in the stump of what once
was the trunk of a pine,
we find a tattered nest...

a story told in twigs and twine,
and in this intricate bundle
of tiny bones.

You say that even after
all these years,
some days you feel
your mother's hand
upon your shoulder.

I tell you that I wake,
rising from dreams,
my brother's music
in my ear.

— Deborah Cooper

MY MOTHER'S STORY

She told the story at some point in every trip we took—her surefire way to keep our interest and pass the time. How they met at fourteen and seventeen, she the older. He, the pastor's son, unnoticed, smitten by her lively, slightly naughty demeanor. How he carried his silent crush through his family's frequent moves; till, at last, in Cheyenne, a thousand or more miles away, at least ten years later, he decided to return to declare his love. And she laughed, said, *Is that what you tell all the girls?* but knew at once from the fall of his face that he was telling his truth. She, five years or more into a dreary engagement, saw herself through his eyes and was immediately gone in her mind from the Nebraska family farm. After less than a year of ardent letters, she left to join him, returning only rarely for visits.

In our young years the romance of her story never faded. It is only now, with both lovers dead, that I find myself trying to reconstruct the story she didn't tell us: how she managed over fifty years to build her life with this kind of man, one who passively, doggedly held on to an adolescent crush for ten years, who never doubted that his love would understand his tardy, surprising return.

— Ann Floreen Niedringhaus

DAY OF THE DEAD

I have read that one should clean the house
for the Day of the Dead
but I don't think
my particular dead
will be deterred
by the disorder in my rooms.
I leave everything
just as it is.

I discuss this at length with the jack-o-lantern
who has been living with me lately.
I will miss the scent of him
when he is gone.
The soft spot on the back of his head
is starting to cave,
his smile beginning
to turn inward.
Sometimes I suspect him
of mocking me in some way,
of looking a little smug
as though he can see through
every pretense in my life
and is about to name names.
Maybe that's not so bad.
Once in awhile one needs
this sort of honesty from a visitor
and we are all just visitors in each other's lives
trying not to overstay our welcomes
or to leave too much of a mess when we go.

We are all just visitors in each other's lives
trying to leave only the memory of light.

I survey my little altar and its treasures.
Every offering I touch
sends a spark and starts a fire
deep in the center of my dry bones.
My dead dance in circles around those fires.
They sing their songs and tell their stories
until the jack-o-lantern caves in completely,
until the hard parts of me
finally soften and fold in on themselves,
get swept away in a current,
in the wild seas and storms and fires
of the great and numinous
disorderly everything.

— Ellie Schoenfeld

LEVIATHAN

Each morning, just past dawn
I'd take the short drive
from home
to your hospital bed.
And, on the way,
listen to the lyrics
of "The Last Leviathan."

What parallels I drew
between a harpooned whale
going down for the last time
and you
I only now recognize:
"And as I take my very last breath."

It is November once again.
The dawn is late,
the days are short –
just as they were
back then.

And, still,
I recall the terrible agonal breaths.
The last shuddering one –
the one where you said
"I love you."

    — Candace Ginsberg

CLEANING HOUSE

Attacking the clutter in the basement
I discover shelves filled with bins
Filled with memories, mysteries, and regrets
    The baby blanket sewn with care –
Blue fleece on one side, funny pictures of new parents on the other
    The yamulka and tefillin from your Bar Mitzvah –
The one your dad bet the house you'd blow
    The rings, necklaces, and pins –
Were they your mom's or from that woman before me?
    The belts – plain leather and bright colored webbing –
Growing longer and longer as the cancer filled your small frame.
    And there, at the very bottom, the Bris cup –
To ease the pain

                     — Candace Ginsberg

TELL ME ABOUT THE STARS

I am forgetting...
forgetting how your hand fit
warm and rough in mine
when we walked out at night,

forgetting how I leaned back
against your shoulder
to look up
as you called the constellations down.

I am forgetting the land sounds –
owl, cricket, spring peepers –
and gentle waves lapping the shore
that bounded our place in the universe.

I have no place now,
I don't find the stars.
Try as I might, I can't believe they are hiding
under clouds that will scatter in due time

or that their light is absorbed
in the splendid glare of sun.
So tell me, please, before I forget:
where are the stars and are you dancing there?

— Anne Simpson

X.

Only that day dawns to which we are awake.

—Henry David Thoreau

THERE IS A RIVER

There is a river that rises
inside of the earth
inside of each of us,
a river flowing with everything
that has ever happened.
Forgotten song lyrics and missing poems
float alongside the spirits of socks
lost in the dryer and the spirits
of our Beloveds who have left
their bodies behind.
They're all in the river.
Everywhere in that river
that connects all rivers,
in that river whose true name
has never been uttered
not even in dreams
though sometimes a syllable
gets caught in a spider's web.
It rushes along
with the cadence of everything
that happens and that doesn't happen
between hello and good-bye.
There are lost earrings in there,
letters that never arrived,
the perfect comeback
that didn't come to you
when you wanted it.

We sit on the banks of that river
and watch the new green unfurling,
the new green nourished
by rivers of sap.
Everything sweet
is in that river,
everything sour
finally worn smooth
in the tumbling that turns time into agates.
Every hurt and humiliation
is washed away.
Our hearts are in that river
and some of us notice
that we are in
way over our heads, swimming with songs
in foreign languages while
sequin-eyed fish shimmer and flit
between the lines.
The river is filled with lost innocence,
with the elusive answers
to the *NY Times* Sunday crossword puzzle,
with the gang-graffiti keyed
into the side of my car,
with Kafka storylines and good jokes.
The river is full of laughs.
The river, like everything else,
is made of stories.
Stories about the roads not taken,
and the sidewalks not shoveled,

about translucent sea creatures,
transparent lies,
transgressions forgiven,
all of it linked verse.
Sacred stories
mix with limericks,
mermaids sing show tunes.

The river passes along our secrets
while dragonflies hover
and sew up loose ends.
The stars and the sun and
the sky's first streaks of morning red
braid and unbraid,
morning and night,
old and young.
Prayers said while kneeling
on rugs, while putting down
tobacco, while sipping wine
and lighting incense
are transubstantiated
and transposed while the Big and Little Dippers
pour the same blessings over all of our heads.
The cathedrals and the strip clubs
are all in that river.
God and the Devil
play poker, the darkness and the light
make love and laugh at us for thinking
that one is different from the other.

Yeats's beast slouches towards Bethlehem
under his Cloths of Heaven
embroidered in light.

Floodwaters and forest fires
raging and burning,
bonfires on beaches
and gale force winds
are all in that river.
The loons and their songs
harmonize with those of the whales. The whales
are wearing Joseph's coat of many colors
and are in a witness protection program.
Our attention spans are in that river
swirling in eddies wishing
for still waters running deep.
Wishbones snap,
peepers sing their traveling songs
for the cold which is running
into the warm and for us,
for all of us who are running and traveling
from one season to the next
spouting off and babbling
while everything else can see
that we are all wet,
just as we should be.

— Ellie Schoenfeld

SOUTH OF DULUTH

A Response to Louis Jenkins

You might be surprised that I could miss seagulls—you who take a leap of faith any time you stroll the Lakewalk bare-headed or toss the crumbs of your sandwich onto the beach, inviting hordes of noisy scavengers to your picnic. But here I am, on the corner of Selby and Western, sitting at a sidewalk café where buses belch diesel fumes into my latte and conversation is interrupted by the wail of sirens and the grinding brakes of garbage trucks. Somewhere, the air is fresh and smells of pine, the horizon holds on to lingering sunsets, and there are quiet evenings when a full moon rises over silver water. Seagulls are primarily a nuisance, I agree, but here in the city—where it seems to tilt dangerously—I count on them to wheel and screech up north, holding the planet in place.

— Anne Simpson

EARLY MARRIAGE
—WEST VIRGINIA

I

The other nurses called them brambles:
prickly creepers climbing up the rock face.
Stopping the car, I gathered
blackberries to make an offering
for you — crystal jelly, all seeds
strained out through a tea towel.
Patients warned me later, *You better
watch out for copperheads on them cliffs.*

You came home from hospital duty,
tired and distracted,
spread my ambrosia thickly and said,
I'd rather have Welch's.

II

To home visits, I drove on
a dry creek bed overhung
with branches and vines.
It ended at a sagging porch,
vacant as the family processed a pig,
newly slaughtered, on the kitchen table.
Drawing me in near the carcass,
folks spoke their maladies: *blind staggers,
drizzlin' shits, a head gatherin'*
that went away with *white lightnin'.*

And you walked home from your shift
in the emergency room
with your own stories: a man impaled
through the chest with a telephone pole,
a woman with a neck goiter the size
of a cantaloupe; a child
whose *smilin' mighty Jesus*
was spinal meningitis.
We talked in the dark before you fell asleep
feeling like Lewis and Clark.

III

Perched on the steepest hill in town,
our house was two stories high on the street,
four stories high in the back.
The gleaming Monongehela River
filled the winding valley bottom far below.

Years later my mother told us,
There was a hole in the bathroom wall.
I worried about rats.
We were surprised.
We couldn't remember a hole.

— Ann Floreen Niedringhaus

HOUSEKEEPING

The goddesses of Autumn shake their mops
till dusty purple asters collect in the ditches,
fluff the clouds on a tight blue sheet of sky,
and pull a golden blanket over the fields.

Taking the hint, we begin to
tuck in for winter –
raking, pruning, covering the garden,
splitting wood and washing windows

in the burst of energy that comes with Indian summer
or in certain seasons of middle age,
then departs without explanation
at the first flake of snow.

— Anne Simpson

PAYING ATTENTION

Carefully I glaze a clay pot. Will I recognize
the pot which is mine after it is fired?

Early in her dementia my mother was frustrated by
what she could not recognize. Later she didn't notice.

Denise Levertov wrote, ... *sometimes I am
hidden from the mountain in veils of inattention.*

All rock and soil in the earth's crust
together make up less than 1 percent of the globe's volume.

I am naturally ambitious and impatient. I have
much to learn from my daughters who have disabilities.

People in many traditional cultures know:
it can be threatening to be observed.

Franz Wright said, ... *everything seen
is something seen for the last time...*

Gradually my daughters learned
to ignore people who stare at them.

The ordinary consoles me. It gives me
visceral knowledge that this has happened before.

Robert Creeley said he learned more about writing poems
from raising chickens than from any university professor.

In his novel, Hesse quotes Siddhartha:
The opposite of every truth is just as true.

My daughters are more capable
of appreciating mystery than I am.

To be absolutely certain in our opinions, we must
ignore the size of the universe, the complexity of a cell.

Sometimes, in sunlight,
I am able to see the iridescence of dust motes

After a long hiatus, the hibiscus
gathers up its juices, spits forth a scarlet bud.

— Ann Floreen Niedringhaus

AWAKE

If you are not called to prayer
five times a day,
if nothing brings you
to your knees

moves you to bow,
to rest your head upon the earth,
this choreography of awe...

if you are not called to prayer
five times a day,
awake,
unstop your ears,
take off the blinders...

a flock of starlings, or
a small fox in a field,
the whisper of the river,
song of rain,
ceiling of stars.

— Deborah Cooper

XI.

The world asks of us
only the strength we have and we give it.
Then it asks for more, and we give it.

— Jane Hirshfield

STILL

The forecast
is for a winter storm.

My first thought
is how
your imbalance
makes it
difficult for you
to walk
on slippery sidewalks,
how your quad canes
sink into snow drifts
making those supports
you lean on
unreliable.

You live
three hours away now.
There is nothing
I can do to protect you.

But still
you are
my first thought
when the forecast
is for a winter storm.

— Ann Floreen Niedringhaus

135

HOME VISIT

Seated in a chair, at last,
her breathing ragged
face grey
I listen to the night crawlers that control her heart.
Writhing, squiggling, the fat worms
create a living net that
holds back the flow of life's blood
and oxygen
from her cells.

A nurse would write:
Temp: 100
Pulse: 120, irregular, bounding
Respirations: 30 per minute, shallow
BP 90/60
O2 at 2 liters per nasal cannula
Skin: warm and dry

"Take these, Mom," I say,
holding out two pills.
"Now, drink this."
"I will be back to check on you."
And in my head, a voice says,
"Not tonight, Mom, not tonight."

I step out her door
into the crisp air.
A porcelain cup moon overhead.
In the distant darkness
the lonely bark of a dog.

— Candace Ginsberg

SOME DAY

Someday –
maybe someday soon –
I shall wake with hope,
ready to get up and move on.
But not today.

So don't tell me that
the sun is warm,
the breeze scented with lilac.
Don't recount my blessings
or remind me to be thankful.

Someday –
maybe someday soon –
I will share your laughter,
tell stories and remember my beloved
as he was.

But today
I'll sit with him and hold his hand,
listen to the shallow ragged breathing,
watch for life to flicker in
sightless eyes,
and wait for a flare of recognition.

          — Anne Simpson

SWIMMING LESSON

Forget that you
    can look through water.
It will hold you.

Forget how your foot
    cleaves it as you step in.
It will carry you.

Forget that each skin molecule
    is caressed by a water molecule,
that each of your cells
    is filled with water.

You were born
    in a gush of water.
It will not dissolve you.

              — Ann Floreen Niedringhaus

POEMS

You find scraps of them in your purse
or a conversation overheard at the store,
in a blurred photograph or a clear insight
when you turn the corner in your car
and the landscape opens itself to you.

You hear phrases of a poem when
you comfort a crying child.

Whole verses write themselves
in the arms of your beloved.

You smell them by the ocean
or in a pine grove after rain,
taste them at dinner with a friend.

Poems lie dormant till you come to your senses
then they sprout a tumble of words...
words that dance circles
all around you,
daring you to pin them to a page.

— Anne Simpson

LET THIS POEM BE

Let this poem be
    an arm around your shoulders
    in the moment that you read this line;
    a hand upon your cheek

    or let it be a shawl
    for this long winter
    spun of willow-green and light.

Let this poem be
    a clearing in a forest;
    now, a torch to ease the night.

Let this poem shape itself
    into a haven;
    make itself a sturdy boat…
    this line, a breeze
    to fill the sail.

Let this poem be a balm.

          — Deborah Cooper

WE COULD BE

We could be
carrying
our only possessions
along an uphill path
as we watch
the horizon
for a cloud of dust
raised by our pursuers.

We could be
applying
pressure
to a spurting wound,
knowing,
as red soaks
through all compresses,
that life can run out.

But we are
holding
the hands
of this hip-high girl
who cannot walk
on her own,
who laughs up at us
in the joy of movement.

— Ann Floreen Niedringhaus

XII.

All know that the drop merges into the ocean
but few know that the ocean merges into the drop.

— Kabir

BEFORE

Sometimes
beginning to burn

a log in the fire will sing,
remembering the birds.

A brown bowl
holding three tangerines

holds too, the memory of
the hands that shaped it

and holds the cool,
still silence
of the earth.

Each tangerine
repeats the image
of the sun.

The shadow
that the rocking chair
releases

dances on the wall
like a tree,
answering the wind.

In the dark
we slip, with the breath,
out of our sleeping bodies

into all we knew before.

— Deborah Cooper

HOPE

My breath lies to me.
It tells me it can go on forever.

Daniel Berrigan said, ... *the more serious the work to be done*
the less one will see of the outcome.

My daughter has significant disabilities.
She first hoped that they would disappear completely.

Lucille Clifton wrote, *We think there's supposed to be*
perfection, as if we understood even what perfection is.

I'm not sure all martyrs have hope.
If not, to what do they cling?

Josephine Jacobsen was stunned by a gravestone inscription:
It's a fearful thing to love what death can touch.

After his wife died in early middle age, the man kept
her body in his basement freezer until he was very elderly.

Viktor Frankl survived Nazi death camps. He reported that
prisoners with a vision for the future were those who survived.

Lepidopterists chase butterflies to mount and label them,
place them in glass boxes stored in drawers.

Berrigan said, *...the good is to be done*
because it is good, not because it goes somewhere.

My daughter's frustrations diminished
when she began to draw.

Shortly before his death Frankl wrote,
Meaning is something to discover rather than to invent.

How old was I when I first understood
the sky is blue behind the gray wall of clouds?

According to James Wright:
It's possible... to live forever in a split second.

The sound of ocean tides
is in the water that washes my hands.

— Ann Floreen Niedringhaus

WHAT I SEND YOU

I send you
this flock of birds
and every dream harbored
under every feather.

I send you this cloud
that dreams of the beach
and looks like a horse galloping hard.

I send you this
quiet field filled
with people asleep
under the ground
who are dreaming about us,
dreaming our lives
into being.

I send you
the very first poem –
the original result
of mixing breathing
with the beating of a heart,
mystery made manifest.
Between the storm
and your skin
there will always be
this poem.

        — Ellie Schoenfeld

PHOENIX

You don't rise on strong, singed wings
you rise wobbly as a hot air balloon,

dipping and soaring,
wafted by the winds of a thousand good-byes

till one day,
high in the thin silence,
you look back clear-eyed
and glimpse the whole shape of things

just before,
through fogged layers of hope,
you begin your descent.

— Anne Simpson

PLUM

The dark plum of summer
sends its final sweetness
running down my chin.
I take one
last
long
bite.
Succulent flesh
bursts forth with glorious indolence,
the hot sun shines
hypnotically
on my face.

Summer stayed late this year
and I am almost
down to the pit, can see
its complicated mazes and ridges.
I worry for a moment
that I will get lost
in those dark alleys.
It looks as dead and inert
as the Autumn all around me
eventually will.
It foreshadows a giving way

to the darkness,
to the deep treasure
and the mystery of the seed.
It swells with the secrets

of how to lie dormant
and then to resurrect,
to fill the world
with flowers,
to recite its seductive poetry of fruit,
to cover the earth in sweet.

— Ellie Schoenfeld

CROSSING OVER

Still
cold
and in the distance
across the grey blue waters
the horizon has blurred –
melded with the winter dark.
And crossing that divide
a lone long ship
with its warm cabin lights
reveals the path it travels
while another, its mere reflection,
marks the place
and space
it has left behind.

— Candace Ginsberg

ABOUT THE POETS

DEBORAH COOPER is the author of five poetry collections, most recently *Under the Influence of Lilacs* published by Clover Valley Press. She co-edited the anthologies *Beloved on the Earth: Poems of Grief & Gratitude* and *The Heart of All That Is: Reflections on Home* (Holy Cow! Press). She is the 2012-2014 Duluth Poet Laureate.

CANDACE GINSBERG, a Duluth native, began writing in the months following her husband's death in 1996 from asbestosis. Soon she was invited to join other poets in their monthly poetry critique meetings—a serious enterprise. The group generously allows Candace to "write little and critique much," but in her dreams, she would like nothing better than to walk the world's beaches and write, write, write.

ANN FLOREEN NIEDRINGHAUS's poems have appeared in numerous regional and national literary journals and in her two chapbooks, *Life Suspended* and *Parallel to the Horizon*. She is assembling her first full-length poetry book, *That Unexplored Terrain*. Ann values her experience of co-teaching poetry writing to inmates at the St. Louis County Jail with Deborah Cooper.

ELLIE SCHOENFELD is a poet from Duluth, Minnesota. Her most recent book is *The Dark Honey: New & Used Poems* (Clover Valley Press), and she has collaborated with various musicians to produce poetry/music CDs. She was co-founder of Poetry Harbor, served on the board of Spirit Lake Poetry Series, and is grateful to the Arrowhead Regional Arts Council for past fellowship support.

ANNE SIMPSON wrote a book with her husband Bob twenty years ago, and recently she published a curriculum for churches based on that book, *Through the Wilderness of Alzheimer's: A Guide in Two Voices*. She has also written a book of poems for Alzheimer's patients called *Growing Down* and has contributed poetry to several journals and anthologies.